ICH HELFE GERN
I LOVE TO HELP

Shelley Admont

Illustriert von Sonal Goyal und Sumit Sakhuja

www.sachildrensbooks.com
Copyright©2016 by S. A. Publishing
innans@gmail.com

All rights reserved. No part of this book may be reproduced in any form or by any electronic or mechanical means, including information storage and retrieval systems, without written permission from the publisher or author, except in the case of a reviewer, who may quote brief passages embodied in critical articles or in a review.

Alle Rechte vorbehalten. Kein Teil dieses Buches darf in irgendeiner Form oder durch irgendwelche elektronischen oder mechanischen Mitteln, einschließlich Informationen Regalbediengeräte schriftlich beim Verlag, mit Ausnahme von einem Rezensenten, kurze Passagen in einer Bewertung zitieren darf reproduziert, ohne Erlaubnis.

First edition, 2016
Translated from Englsih by Tess Parthum
Aus dem Englischen übersetzt von Tess Parthum

I Love to Help (German English Bilingual Edition)/ Shelley Admont
ISBN: 978-1-5259-0191-1 paperback
ISBN: 978-1-5259-0192-8 hardcover
ISBN: 978-1-5259-0190-4 eBook

Please note that the German and English versions of the story have been written to be as close as possible. However, in some cases they differ in order to accommodate nuances and fluidity of each language.

Although the author and the publisher have made every effort to ensure the accuracy and completeness of information contained in this book, we assume no responsibility for errors , inaccuracies, omission, inconsistency, or consequences from such information.

Für die, die ich am meisten liebe—S.A.
For those I love the most—S.A.

Jimmy sprang aufgeregt um das Auto herum.
Jimmy bounced around the car in excitement.

„Wir fahren zum Strand!", rief er glücklich. „Wir fahren zum Strand!"
"We're going to the beach!" he shouted happily.
"We're going to the beach!"

Papa lachte, als er den Kofferraum des Autos öffnete. „Das stimmt!", sagte er. „Es ist ein herrlicher, sonniger Tag und wir sollten uns schnell auf den Weg machen."
Dad laughed as he opened the trunk of the car. "That's right!" he said, "It's a lovely sunny day and we want to get going quickly."

„Warum hilfst du uns nicht, die Sachen, die wir brauchen, zum Auto zu tragen? Deine Brüder helfen schon."
"Why don't you help us carry the things we need to the car? Your brothers are helping already."

Jimmy hörte auf zu springen und schaute zur Eingangstür ihres Hauses.

Jimmy stopped bouncing and looked towards the front door of their house.

Jimmys Brüder halfen gerade dabei, die Sachen zum Auto zu tragen.

Jimmy's two brothers were helping carry things to the car.

Der älteste Bruder hatte bunte Eimer und Spaten in den Händen und der mittlere Bruder trug den Picknickkorb.

The oldest brother had colorful buckets and spades in his hands, and the middle brother was carrying the picnic basket.

„Komm, Jimmy!", rief Mama vom Eingang aus. „Du kannst die Tasche mit den Handtüchern oder diesen kleinen Liegestuhl tragen. Das ist gar nicht schwer."
"Come, Jimmy!" Mom called from the doorway. "You can carry the bag of towels or this small beach chair. It won't be very hard."

Jimmy sah die Handtücher und den Stuhl an. „Nein, danke!", sagte er grinsend. „Ich bin zu sehr mit SPRINGEN beschäftigt!"
Jimmy looked at the towels and chair. "No, thank you!" he said with a grin. "I'm too busy JUMPING!"

Der Wald, in dem sie wohnten, war nicht allzu weit vom Strand entfernt, und Jimmy zappelte auf dem ganzen Weg vor Aufregung.

The forest where they lived was not too far from the beach and Jimmy wriggled with excitement the whole way.

Als er den goldenen Sand des Strandes und das glitzernde blaue Wasser des Meeres sah, fing er an, auf seinem Sitz zu hüpfen.

When he saw the golden sands of the beach and the sparkling blue water of the sea, he started jumping in his seat.

„So, wir sind da", sagte Papa. „Lasst uns aussteigen und den Tag genießen!"

"Alright, we are here," said Dad. "Let's get out and enjoy the day!"

Jimmy stieg aus dem Auto aus. „Das ist unglaublich!", schrie er und rannte auf das Wasser zu.

Jimmy got out of the car. "This is amazing," he exclaimed and ran down towards the water.

„Warte!", rief Mama ihm hinterher. „Du musst uns helfen, alles aus dem Auto zu holen."

"Wait!" Mom called after him. "You've got to help us to take everything out of the car."

Jimmy drehte sich um und winkte seiner Familie zu. „Nein, danke!", sagte er. „Ich muss eine RIESIGE SANDBURG bauen!"

Jimmy turned around, waving at his family. "No, thank you!" he said. "I've got to build a GIANT SANDCASTLE!"

Er rannte zu einer perfekten Stelle am Strand, direkt neben dem Meer, und fing an, Sand mit seinen Händen zu schaufeln.

He ran to a perfect spot on the beach, right next to the sea, and started to scoop sand into his hands.

Jimmy war so beschäftigt, dass er nicht bemerkte, wie seine Familie zum Auto und zurück lief und Sachen zum Strand hinunter trug.

Jimmy was so busy that he didn't notice his family going to and from the car, carrying objects down to the beach.

In der Zwischenzeit wurde seine Sandburg größer und größer.

Meanwhile, the sandcastle grew bigger and bigger.

„Meine Burg wird so groß sein, dass ein König und eine Königin darin einziehen wollen!", sagte Jimmy und stellte sich winzige Ritter und Diener vor, die darin umherliefen.

"My castle is going to be so big, a King and Queen are going to want to move in!" Jimmy said, imagining tiny knights and servants running around inside.

Während Jimmy an seiner Burg arbeitete, suchten seine älteren Brüder nach der größten Muschel, die sie finden konnten.

While Jimmy was working on his castle, his older brothers were hunting for the biggest shell they could find.

Papa ging im Meer schwimmen und Mama lag weiter oben am Strand auf ihrem Handtuch.

Dad went swimming in the sea and Mom lay on a towel further up the beach.

Jimmy war so auf seine Burg konzentriert, dass er nicht wirklich bemerkte, was der Rest seiner Familie machte, bis...

Jimmy was so focused on his castle that he didn't really notice what the rest of his family were doing until...

„Pass auf!", hörte Jimmy seinen Papa rufen.
"Watch out!" Jimmy heard his dad shout.

Er schaute gerade rechtzeitig auf, um eine riesige Welle zu sehen, die sich neben ihm aus dem Meer auftürmte!
He looked up just in time to see a giant wave rising up beside him from the sea!

„Oh nein!", schrie Jimmy, als die Welle sich auf ihn stürzte. Als sich das Wasser zurückzog, lag Jimmy auf seinem Rücken und versuchte durchzuatmen.
"Oh no!" cried Jimmy as the wave crashed down on top of him. When the water pulled away, Jimmy lay on his back and tried to catch his breath.

„Igitt!" Jimmy spuckte Salzwasser aus und zog Seegras hinter seinen Ohren hervor.
"Yuck!" Jimmy spat out salty water and pulled seaweed from behind his ears.

Dann sah er auf, um nachzusehen, was mit seiner Burg passiert war.

Then he looked up to see what had happened to his castle.

„Nein!", schrie er. Die Burg war vollständig zerstört!

"Noooo!" he cried. The castle was completely destroyed!

Jimmy spürte heiße Tränen auf seinem Gesicht, als er die zerstörte Burg ansah.

Jimmy felt hot tears on his face as he looked at the ruined castle.

Mama kniete sich neben ihn und umarmte ihn. Seine ganze Familie hatte mit dem aufgehört, was sie gerade tat, und versammelte sich um ihn herum.

Mom knelt down beside him and gave him a hug. All his family had stopped what they were doing and gathered around him.

„Das mit deiner Burg tut mir leid", sagte Papa.
"I'm sorry about your castle," Dad said.

„Ja, sie sah richtig toll aus", sagte sein ältester Bruder.
"Yeah, it looked really cool," said the oldest brother.

„Und groß", stimmte der mittlere Bruder zu.
"And big," agreed the middle brother.

Mama lächelte. „Keine Sorge, Jimmy. Wir werden dir helfen, eine neue zu bauen."
Mom smiled. "Don't worry, Jimmy. We'll help you build a new one."

„Das werdet ihr?", fragte Jimmy.
"You will?" Jimmy asked.

„Ja!" Seine Familie lachte und sie machten sich alle daran, die Sandburg wieder aufzubauen.
"Yes!" His family laughed and they all set about building the sandcastle again.

Diesmal war etwas anders. Jimmy erkannte, dass die Burg mit der Hilfe seiner Familie größer und schöner war als zuvor.

Something was different this time. Jimmy realized that with his family helping him, the castle was bigger and more beautiful than before.

Als sie fertig waren, war es die größte Sandburg, die Jimmy jemals gesehen hatte!

By the time they were finished, it was the biggest sandcastle Jimmy had ever seen!

„Schau!", zeigte der älteste Bruder hinein. Zwei Krabben hatten sich im Zentrum der Burg niedergelassen. „Es gibt sogar einen König und eine Königin!"

"Look!" the oldest brother pointed inside. Two crabs had settled down in the center of the castle. "It even has a King and Queen!"

Jimmy hüpfte auf und ab. „Das ist die beste Sandburg aller Zeiten!"

Jimmy bounced up and down. "This is the best sandcastle ever!"

Als es Zeit war zu gehen, begann die Familie, die Sachen wieder ins Auto zu bringen.
When it was time to go, the family began taking things back into the car.

Jimmy grinste. „Kann ich euch helfen?", fragte er.
Jimmy grinned. "May I help you?" he asked.

Er brachte die Handtücher zum Auto und rannte dann zurück, um dabei zu helfen, auch die Eimer und Spaten zu tragen.
He took the towels to the car and then ran back to help carry the buckets and spades too.

„Mensch, das haben wir richtig schnell eingepackt", sagte Papa, als sie fertig waren, und sah den leeren Strand an.
"Wow, we packed that really quickly," Dad said when they were done, looking at the empty beach.

Selbst als sie nach Hause kamen, half Jimmy weiter und trug die Liegestühle zurück ins Haus.

Even when they came home, Jimmy continued to help, carrying the beach chairs back into the house.

„Alles funktioniert besser, wenn wir uns gegenseitig helfen", sagte er zu Mama.

"Everything works out better when we help each other," he told Mom.

Mama lächelte. „Nun, das Auto ist jetzt leer - mit einer Ausnahme."

Mom smiled. "Well, the car is empty now, except for one thing."

Mama holte eine Packung Kekse heraus. „Ich glaube, jemand muss dabei helfen, diese Kekse zu essen!"

Mom pulled out a packet of cookies. "I think someone needs to help eat these cookies!"

www.ingramcontent.com/pod-product-compliance
Lightning Source LLC
LaVergne TN
LVHW072104060526
838200LV00061B/4806